I0439733

How to Draw Dinosaurs

(A step- by- step guide to draw Triceratops, Stegosaurus, Tarbosaurus and many many more)

By Alex Man

Book 2

Table of Contents:

Triceratops ——————————

Ornitholestes ——————————

Suchomimus ——————————

Stegosaurus ——————————

Telmatosaurus ——————————

stenopelix ——————————

Struthiomimus ——————————

staurikosaurus ——————————

Minmi ——————————

Tarbosaurus

Sinornithosaurus

Psittacosaurus

Rebbachisaurus

Prosaurolophus

Lophostropheus

Spinosaurus

Coelophysis

Stegoceras

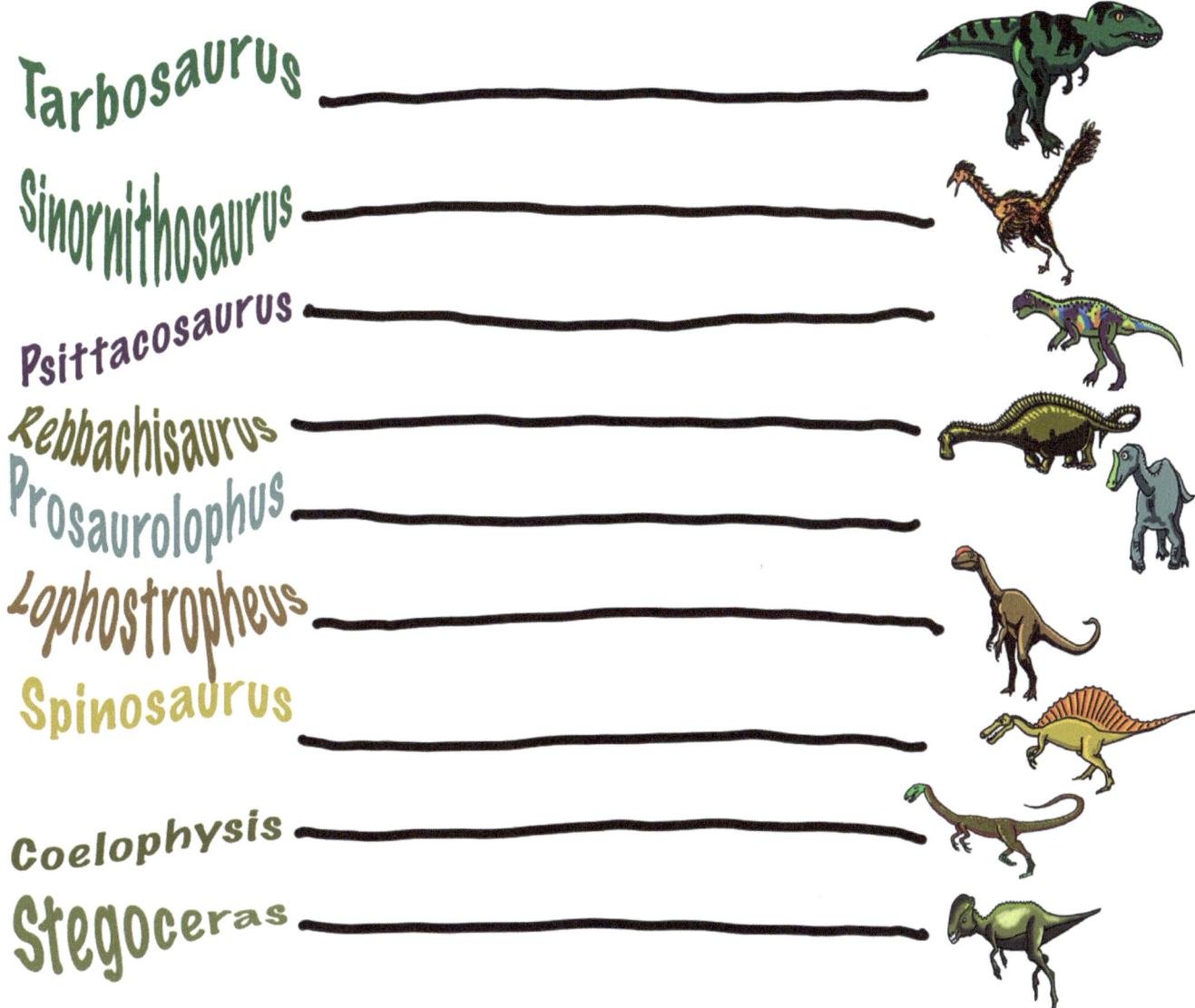

Everyone can draw!
Drawing is like music, a universal language.
In this book I will show you,
step by step,
how to draw dinosaurs.

The instructions are given only by drawings,
so there is no need to add text,
that way even young children
can use the book by themselves.

On each page you can find a different dinosaur.
On one page you have the directions on how to draw,
and on the following page the drawing with its environment,
as a part of the whole picture.

I put a lot of effort into this book,
trying to make the drawings easy,
and accessible for all, and most importantly- fun for all!
I hope you will enjoy both learning how to draw the dinosaurs
and the experience.
So... grab a sheet of paper and a pencil,
and let's go back in time into the world of dinosaurs.
Sincerely yours,
Alex

Triceratops

Ornitholestes

Suchomimus

Stegosaurus

Telmatosaurus

Stenopelix

Struthiomimus

Staurikosaurus

Minmi

Tarbosaurus

Sinornithosaurus

Psittacosaurus

Rebbachisaurus

Prosaurolophus

Lophostropheus

Spinosaurus

Coelophysis

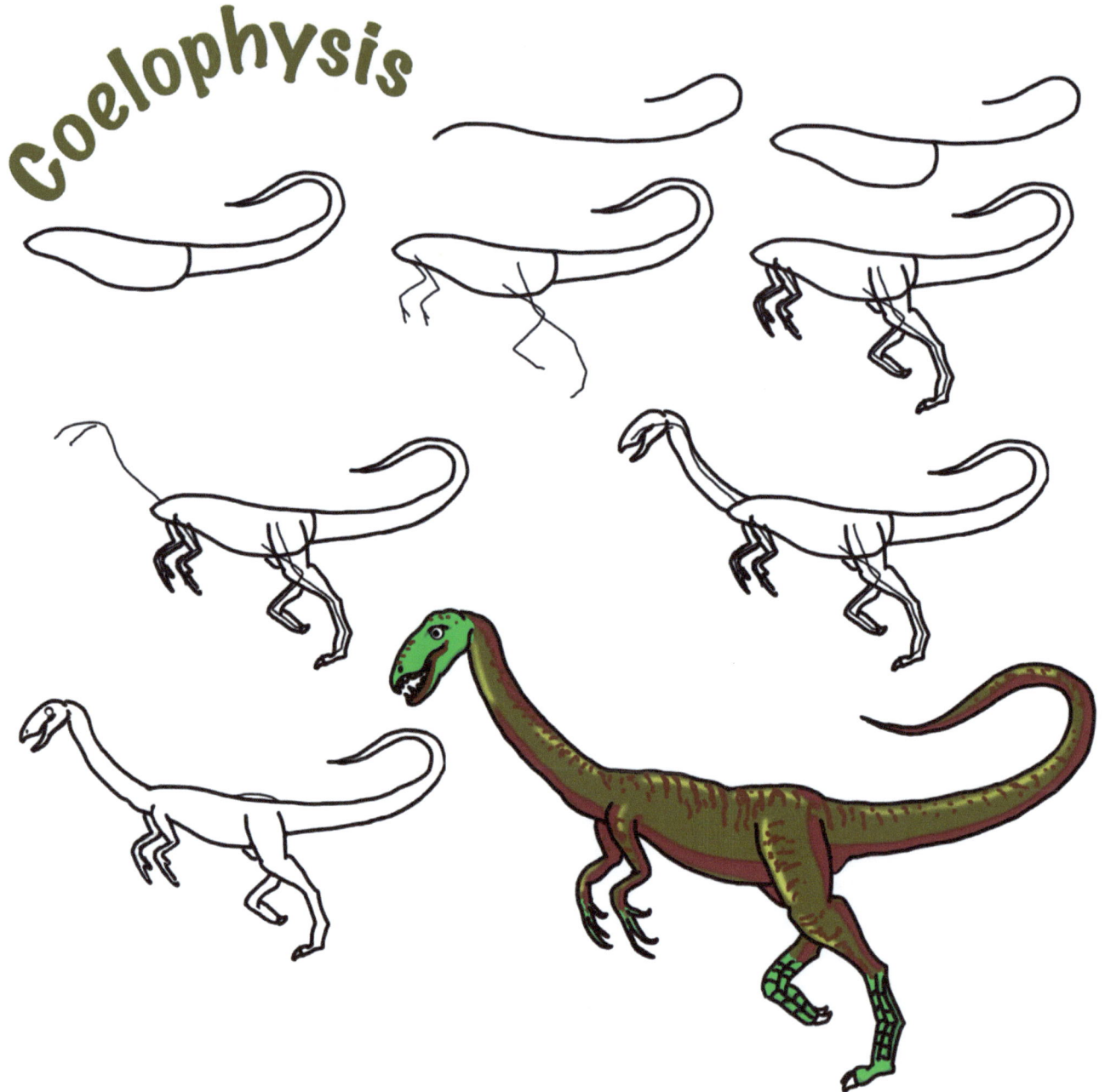

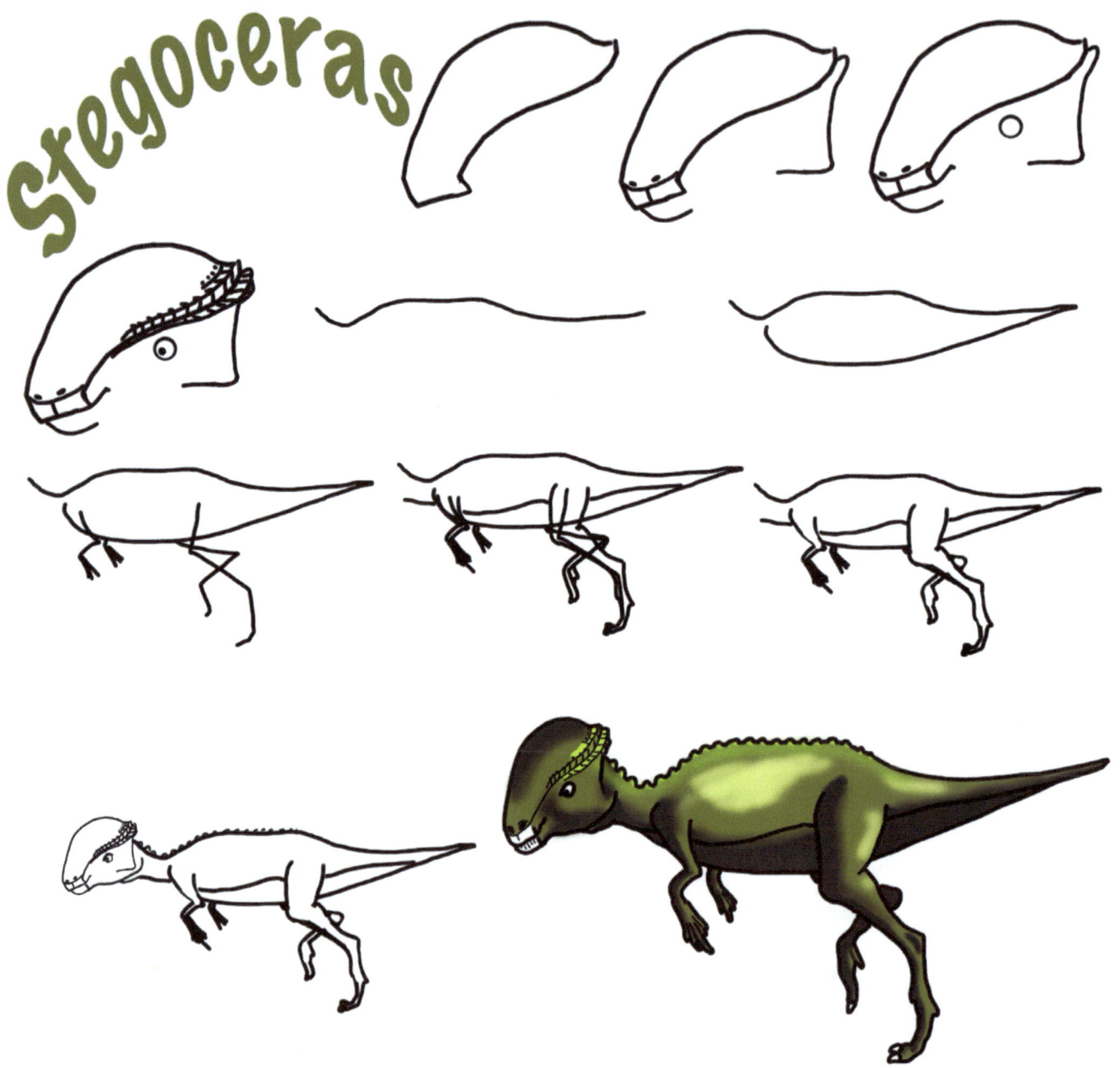

Stegoceras